Ellerslie Wallace

A Descriptive Reading on Switzerland

Ellerslie Wallace

A Descriptive Reading on Switzerland

ISBN/EAN: 9783337155575

Printed in Europe, USA, Canada, Australia, Japan

Cover: Foto ©ninafisch / pixelio.de

More available books at **www.hansebooks.com**

A

DESCRIPTIVE READING

ON

SWITZERLAND

ILLUSTRATED BY FIFTY LANTERN
SLIDES

BY ELLERSLIE WALLACE

WILLIAM H. RAU
PHILADELPHIA
1890

ILLUSTRATIONS.

SWITZERLAND.

In EXHIBITING our series of fifty views of Switzerland, we shall undoubtedly interest those of our friends who have never visited this beautiful land. We make this very positive assertion because the scenic resources of this wonderful country cannot be exhausted by any series of mountain views, though these are the chief attraction. The cities and villages, the great engineering works, and last, but not least, the mighty glaciers, offer so much of pictorial interest that we have introduced a liberal number of each. We feel that this selection will serve to give a good general idea of the land of Switzerland, and afford a pleasant variety.

Those who have been fortunate enough to make a trip through this country, "where every prospect pleases," will recognize many familiar places. Having arranged our views in about the order in which they would be seen by anyone traveling over the usual route, we may begin by looking at some of the cities.

1. Panorama of Bale.—This beautiful and very characteristic Swiss town has sometimes been called the "Key to the Alps." It is finely situated on the River Rhine, in the northern part of Switzerland, where the country is not mountainous, but quite pastoral and gentle in character, when compared with the ruggedness of the southern districts.

The town is divided into two parts by the Rhine, which flows swiftly along, and brings with it a delicious coolness from the mighty glaciers of the higher Alps.

Our view is taken from the smaller section of the town, or " Little Bale," as it is called, looking across the Rhine and the old bridge to the main part of the city. The celebrated hotel of " The Three Kings " is seen at the right of the view.

Bale is a wealthy and conservative old place. It still presents many of the features of the mediæval German city, and is the abode of numerous retired merchants and people of means. On account of these picturesque features in the street architecture it is worthy of being visited, and is a fitting entry into the glories of the mountain region farther south. Our view gives a good idea of the river front, but, as is often the case in these old towns, the streets are too narrow for good photographing to be done in them.

Contenting ourselves with this general panorama of Bale, we will now visit the town of Zurich.

2. Zurich From the Quaibrucke.—The situation of this beautiful city is quite different from that of Bale, as it stands at the foot of the lake of Zurich, just on its outlet, as the River Limmat is called.

Our picture has been taken from the Quai Bridge, the southernmost one of the six which cross the Lim- mat, and it stands directly upon the lake. We see how picturesquely the town is built on both sides of the Limmat, and can see one of the pretty modern bridges connecting the two portions in the middle distance. The town is well supplied with churches. We see the two towers of the Gross Munster at the right, and the very picturesque spire of the Frau Munster at the left. We also observe the Town Library (which con- tains some valuable antiquities), in a small building looking like a chapel, and the pretty Sonnenquai, well shaded with trees, over to the right, near the Gross Munster. The river baths, which are a feature of all the larger Swiss towns, are seen on the left as a pair of long, low buildings. The constant influx of an immense quantity of clear, fresh water renders these baths very delightful, and they are largely patronized.

The church of St. Peter, seen on the left, just beyond the Frau Munster, was presided over for more than twenty years by Lavater. The celebrated Zwingli was incumbent of the Gross Munster from 1519 to 1531. Zurich is a bustling and active centre of manufacturing industry in cotton and silk goods; it is also celebrated for its schools, and may be called the chief centre of the intellect of German Switzerland.

3. Zurich. The Bridge and Lake.—Changing our position a little, we now get a good view of the splendid Quai Bridge on which we stood while photographing our last view. We observe the plain, yet substantial manner in which the bridge is built, and the ample space provided for vehicles and for footpassengers. We must ask our friends in the audience to take our word for it that the water which runs under the five spans of the bridge is clear, and of the most beautiful light green tint, quite different from the rivers seen in most places where there is as much manufacturing going on as there is in Zurich.

The pretty and attractive character of the suburbs of Zurich can be seen in some degree on the left of the view, beyond the bridge. The country is beautifully diversified with copses of trees, well-built houses and institutions, and water-courses; the background being filled in with hills, often of considerable height.

Much interesting matter, in the shape of historical reminiscences of the Reformation is to be found in this quaint, yet beautiful city. We could spend a good deal of time profitably here, but must hurry on to the south on our way to the mountains.

4. Swiss Chalets.—The interesting features of Switzerland are not confined either to its great mountain ranges or to its wealthy and picturesque cities. Our route from Zurich to Lucerne takes us through a beautiful pastoral district, where we often see the evidences of considerable wealth, while again, we pass through small hamlets, where the inhabitants are of the poorest class.

Our picture shows us one of these villages where the people are all in very modest circumstances, but live in houses or "chalets," as they are sometimes called, that are so pretty that we cannot pass them by without notice.

A leading characteristic of these chalets is that they are strongly built. The foundations and the walls are of stone, well laid, and, as in the view before us, whitened with lime. There is considerable room under the broad projecting eaves that is utilized for storing away farm implements of various kinds. There is by no means so much room in the interior of the chalet itself. The families as a rule are large, and there is much crowding. We see that the supply of wood for cooking purposes has been neatly piled near the door, where it gets the full force of the sun's heat to keep it dry, the overhanging eaves at the same time protecting it in great degree against the rain. The eaves of the stables and cow-houses belonging to this chalet can be seen on the right hand. Across the road, and at a short distance beyond, we observe one of the imposing turreted houses, which are not uncommon in the older Swiss villages. The large chalet at the left was probably built before the road was laid out, as can be seen from the angular direction in which it stands to the line of the road.

5. Lucerne. The Old Lantern and Bridge.—The City of Lucerne, at the foot of the lake of the same name, or as it is sometimes called, "The Lake of the Four Cantons," is one of the most charming in Europe, just as the lake is one of the most picturesque and beautiful. Although the grander and wilder scenery of the lake is found near its head, as we shall see in a few minutes, it may well be asked whether the surroundings of the City of Lucerne are not equally interesting in their way, the open reaches of the lake near the city affording views of the fine mountain ranges that cannot be had in the narrower parts at the foot.

Our view is taken from the Theatre Quai, looking across the outlet of the lake or River Reuss, to the older portion of the town. The large tower is called the water-tower or lantern and is a well-preserved relic of the ancient fortifications of the town; a part of these old ramparts is also to be seen on the hill back of the city. Some historians claim that the present name of the town—Lucerne, has been taken from this tower in the view before us, which in Latin was called *lucerna*,—a light-house, and was formerly used as such. It is now a depostory for some of the archives of the city.

The long, dark line crossing the picture just in the rear of the tower is one of the curiosities of the place, and is known as the "Capellbrucke." This stanch old bridge was built as long ago as the year 1303, and, in like manner with the Muhlenbrucke, a little farther down the stream, contains a number of quaint old paintings, supported on the braces just under the roof. There are seventy-seven of these pictures in the Capellbrucke, and they represent various episodes in the lives of St. Maurice and St. Leger, the patrons of the city.

A promenade on this bridge is delightful on a warm summer's day ; the water runs with great swiftness, creating a cool refreshing breeze, and is of a fine emerald green color.

6. The Lake Front, Lucerne.—Our way from the quaint old Capellbrucke to the garden where the great carving of the lion, by Thorwaldsen is, takes us naturally along the lake front of the city. There are few walks in Europe more charming than this one. We can choose between the splendid pavements immediately under the great hotels, with attractive shop windows at every step, and the more shaded walk under the double row of fine linden trees. This is seen as a dark line crossing the whole breadth of the picture, just above the water-line, and concealing the lower stories of the hotels. Should we choose the latter route we shall certainly admit that the views over the lake—the most beautiful in this beautiful land—with the traffic of the street just at a pleasant distance, and the interest we feel in watching foreign life and manners, both on the water and on shore, combine to render our promenade along the lake front of Lucerne something to remember forever.

Indeed we can well afford, in imagination, to seat ourselves upon one of the numerous benches under the close-clipped, yet thickly-leaved lindens, and watch the steamers as they arrive from Fluelen, Brunnen, Vitznau, and other picturesque points on the lake, and follow the motley groups of sight-seers as they land and make the best of their way to the Schweizerhof, the National, or some other hotel. Tourists from all parts of the world will here be seen, and as we have before hinted, they are not the least interesting feature to be observed in a trip in Switzerland.

The famous Schweizerhof Hotel, certainly unsurpassed, and perhaps unequalled in the world, stands on the other side of the linden trees, about in the centre of the view. The towers in the rear are on the old wall, back of the city; are very well preserved, dating from the fourteenth century.

7. Thorwaldsen's Lion, Lucerne.— Compared with other cities and towns of Europe, Lucerne cannot boast of much in the way of objects of art. Apart from some ancient specimens of stained glass and a fine organ in the Cathedral there is but one attraction; this one however, is unique, and has a world-wide celebrity. The figure of a lion in the agonies of death cut out in the face of a sandstone rock immediately above a sequestered pool of water is so entirely out of the common, so striking, and so weird in

effect, that we can well understand the interest it
excites even in those who have never seen it.

Let us say, that a good photograph, such as we
here have before us, gives a far better idea of this
beautiful monument than any model no matter how
well made.

This colossal figure is a monument to the memory of
the Swiss Guards who bravely defended the Royal
Family of France at the Tuilleries in Paris from the
attacks of the mob, during the Revolution of 1792.
The lion, wounded to the death, is seen protecting a
shield with the Bourbon lilies by means of his paw.
The carving is magnificently done in a manner quite
worthy of the exacted nobility of the design. Thorwaldsen's original model may still be seen in a shop
not far away from the place; and we must not omit to
mention the name of Ahorn of Constance who per-
formed the difficult labor of carving the great figure
out of the living rock.

Its dimensions are twenty-eight feet in length by
eighteen in height. The names of the officers who
perished are cut on the rock just below, and are often-
times partially concealed by the ferns and creeping
plants. These frequently become tinged with various
colors from frost, when the effect is even more picturesque.

It is now time for us to start on our trip up the lake
towards the great Saint Gotthard, and our first stop
will be at the

8. Hotel on the Rigi Kulm, Lake of Lucerne.
—There is, perhaps, no other mountain in the world
so often visited as the Rigi. Our own Mount Washington in New Hampshire is the greatest rival of the

Rigi in point of numbers of visitors, being one of the few instances in which there is direct railway communication to the summit from large cities.

The Rigi Kulm or summit is reached by a railway very similar to that on Mount Washington, the ascent being one foot in every four, and the same arrangement of toothed wheels and rails employed. The speed is about three miles per hour. Charming views are obtained on the way up, the interest increasing as the train proceeds.

The Rigi Kulm is an open plateau of considerable size covered with grass and walks an elevation of 5931 feet above sea-level, thus being higher than any mountain in Great Britain. The height above the Lake of Lucerne is 4478 feet. In the picture, the Kulm is at the left, some distance beyond the hotel.

During the summer season the hotel is crowded to overflowing, particularly in the mornings and evenings. The sunsets and sunrises are the chief attraction; a horn being blown every clear morning at about four o'clock to awaken the guests in time for the rising. The views of the great snowy peaks of Switzerland, and of the lakes of Lucerne and Zug at the mountain's foot, are wonderfully fine.

The value of land even at this great height is more than might be imagined. It is stated that the plot of ground measuring 96 x 55 feet, on which the hotel is built, cost $10,000.

9. Old Cottages at Gersau, Lake of Lucerne.— Continuing our sail up the lake towards Fluelen, we stop for a moment at the characteristic and pretty village of Gersau, which lies at the foot of one of the spurs of the Rigi.

The village together with a very small patch of land including not more than six square miles, was once an independent State, and continued so for four hundred years. Murray's Guide to Switzerland gives the following historical account: "The people of Gersau bought their freedom in 1390 with a sum of 690 pounds of pfennigs, scraped together after years of hard toil to satisfy the Lords of Moos, citizens of Lucerne, whose serfs they had previously been. They maintained their independence apart from any canton, and were governed by a landamanan and council, chosen from among themselves, until the French occupied Switzerland in 1798, since which they have been united with canton Schwyz. Though Gersau possessed a criminal jurisdiction of its own, together with a gallows long left standing, no instance of a capital execution occurred during the whole of its existence as a separate State."

The cottage or chalet in the middle of the picture is a fair specimen of the older style of plain Swiss wooden house. The white portion at the bottom is stone coated with lime ; all the upper part, however, is of wood. The house at the right is of stone throughout. By looking closely at the former, we can see the overhanging stories and projecting eaves that give these older Swiss chalets such a comfortable and picturesque appearance. The wood not being painted, turns a fine deep brown color with age, and contrasts beautifully with the white walls below and the green trees surrounding it.

10. The Axenstrasse and the Alps, Lake of Lucerne.—This famous road gives the traveler a fine opportunity of seeing the scenery all along the Bay of Uri, as this portion of the lake is named, and which is remarkable for its grand steep mountain-sides. The lake narrows rapidly until it comes to its head at Fluelen, the little town seen just at the base of the high cone-shaped mountain with the snow on its top. The Axenstrasse, which in the picture is seen to be several hundred feet above the water, descends to the town and then continues on through Altdorf, Amsteg and other villages to Andermatt and Hospenthal, making a rapid ascent on the way.

On the opposite side of the lake, a short distance above the spot where our view is taken, is the Rutli, or meadow, where the Swiss patriots took oath to fight their enemies to the last (November 7th, 1307); and not far away is a large isolated rock in the lake, with an inscription to the German poet, Schiller.

The charming view before us represents one of the great engineering feats in the matter of road construction, together with the beautiful landscape for which, when combined, Switzerland is justly famous. The Lake of Lucerne, or lake of the four forest cantons of Uri, Schwyz, Unterwalden and Lucerne, is very irregular in shape but surrounded by lofty mountains, particularly in that portion where our view is made. The half-historical, half-mythical legend of William Tell and the apple is located near this spot, where a rustic chapel on the lake shore was built in commemoration of the hero by the Canton of Uri in 1388.

Let us now go a short distance down the road towards the tunnel or gallery as they call it.

11. Gallery of the Axenstrasse, looking towards Fluelen.—We can get from this picture some idea of the immense amount of work laid out on this splendid road, and of the noble views of the lake and mountains which it affords. The portion shown in the view is a "gallery" or half-tunnel; the road running so near the surface of the rock that the outer portions have been broken away leaving a sort of roof overhead. The continuation of the road, through a tunnel where it pierces more deeply into the rock, is seen at the extreme left of the picture.

An uncommon place like this would command attention anywhere on account of its peculiar construction, but the magnificent views from the openings of the gallery confer an interest upon it that is unique. It must be remembered that we are now at the head of the Lake of Lucerne, and surrounded by the steep rocky mountains which, as before remarked, close it in. Anyone standing near the stone guards below the openings so as to be able to have an unobstructed view could see the Uri-Rothstock and other fine mountains opposite ; from our present standpoint we can see the symmetrical Bristenstock in the distance, and by looking closely, a few whitish spots which mark the situation of the town of Fluelen, at which we will take a closer look in our next slide. It will be observed that we are high above the waters of the lake, a fact which adds materially to the picturesque interest of the locality.

12. Fluelen.—We may now imagine that we have continued on through the tunnel seen in our last view, and descended several hundreds of feet, until we are almost upon the level of the water, and quite close to the town of Fluelen. There are few towns in Switzerland so beautifully situated, and surrounded by such imposing and lovely natural scenery.

This view has been taken in precisely the same direction as the preceding one, the only difference being, as we have already said, that we are lower down, and somewhat nearer the town. The symmetrical Bristenstock, with its snow-covered sides, which we saw from the gallery a few moments ago, we now see again, right in the centre of the picture, with its peak lost in the gathering storm clouds. Other high mountains are seen on the right and left, which were hidden by the stonework of the gallery in our former view.

There is no interest connected to Fluelen apart from its beautiful situation and surroundings. Our picture is a characteristic bit of the truly ideal Swiss landscape. The finely cultivated grass-fields, the pretty, neat houses and well-kept roads, the tall poplar trees, and the noble lake at the foot of the superb snow-capped mountains, together form an *ensemble* which we may well call "Picturesque Fluelen."

A few miles further on, brings us to the

13. Saint Gotthard Tunnel, at Goschenen.—It might not at first be supposed that the picture now on the screen represents one of the triumphs of modern engineering. We here have a view of the northern or Swiss end of the great tunnel which underlies the old St. Gotthard stage or diligence route. It was built in order that direct rail communication might be made between Italy and Switzerland ; the ends being respectively at Airolo in the former, and at Goschenen in the latter country. Its total length between the points named is nine and a quarter miles. The cost was $11,350,000. The work was begun in

June, 1872, on the Swiss side, the point seen in our view. About four weeks after, the work was similarly started on the Italian side, and was continued for nearly eight years, being finished February 29th, 1880. The number of workmen employed per day varied from twenty-five hundred to thirty-four hundred.

The tunnel is twenty-eight feet wide, and twenty-one feet in height. It is finished in stone and is well supplied with fresh air. There is a double line of tracks throughout. The express time for passing through the tunnel is sixteen minutes.

The stream of water seen to the right is the River Reuss, which here makes a very repid descent. The cloudy appearance at the tunnel's mouth in the centre of the picture is smoke from a train that has just entered.

Although business is much facilitated by the tunnel, the traveler passing through it is compelled to forego the magnificent scenery of the St. Gotthard Pass, which is ranked by many as one of the finest passes in Switzerland for views.

14. The Saint Gotthard Pass.—The picture now on the screen gives a good idea of that portion of the Saint Gotthard stage-roufe lying just below the Devil's Bridge, which forms the subject of our next view. The exceedingly wild and precipitous slopes of the hills on either side of the route are plainly distinguishable, and render it easy to imagine the necessity of protecting the road against the slides and avalanches that are of very frequent occurence in this region. One of the graceful serpentine loops made by the road as it descends is seen in the foreground of the view, a small portion at the bottom not being included. By following the road as it proceeds along the left bank of the stream, one of the avalanche tunnels is seen, its entrance looking like a semi-circular black spot, and small in size, owing to its distance from the camera. By looking more closely the tunnel is seen to be of some considerable length, and very strongly built to prevent the landslides which rush down here from doing damage to it. A still closer examination shows a small stream of water tumbling down the mountain side, on the rough rocks left by the last landslide, and after crossing the roof of the tunnel, proceeding to join the River Reuss below. The latter can be seen in the lower middle portion of the picture for a small portion of its course; the road is situated higher and to the left, and although narrower, can be more plainly distinguished. The scenery increases in wildness as we ascend to the Devil's Bridge, which may be said to be the culminating point of interest of the route.

At the commencement of this century the road was a mere bridle-path, the work of constructing a regular carriage-way not being completed until 1832. The old route was much traveled; it has been estimated that sixteen thousand persons and nine thousand horses crossed the pass every year. So far as transportation of freight is concerned, the railroad which lies underneath, and of which we had a view in our last slide, has already superseded the carriage-way; travelers of all classes, however, who are not pressed for time, will prefer the open stage-route for the sake of the fine views, and avoid the long, smoky, dark passage of the tunnel.

15. Saint Gotthard Pass.—The Devil's Bridge. —We have here a fair view of the most picturesque portion of the Pass. The River Reuss descends with such quickness as to form a sort of lengthened cascade, and also makes a sharp bend to the right to get around the enormous rocky precipice, the bottom of which is seen in the right-hand upper corner of the picture. The roadway, of which a small portion can be seen at the right, lower down, has been blasted out of the solid rock. The new bridge is a fine granite structure, with a single arch of twenty-six feet span, and erected in 1830. The old bridge, seen just below it, is no longer used.

The wild and romantic surroundings of this spot never fail to strike the attention of travelers, but there is also a melancholy interest attached to the bridge and and to the "Urner Loch," which is a short tunnel just above to the left, great loss of life having taken place there in 1799, in a battle between the French, Austrians and Russians. "On the morning of September 25th, the Russians forced the passage of the Urner Loch with severe loss, but were again checked at the Devil's Bridge, which was stoutly defended by the French. The latter attempted to blow up the bridge, but only succeeded in destroying a stone embankment by which it was approached. Nothing daunted, the Russians gallantly descended, under galling fire to the bed of the Reuss, succeeded in crossing it, and clambering up the opposite bank, after a fierce conflict compelled their enemy to retreat to the Lake of Lucerne."

After passing through the tunnel, a short distance brings us out into the mountain valley of Urseren. Passing through to Andermatt, we arrive at

16. Hospenthal.—This characteristic Swiss village is situated in the Ursersen valley, near the junction of the roads leading to the Vurka Pass, and the St. Gotthard route, which we have thus far followed from the Lake of Lucerne. It stands at the high elevation of 4,800 feet, and is noted for its invigorating and pure atmosphere; not quite so cold as at the summit of the pass, but just as bracing.

In fine weather nothing is more delightful than a stay in this locality, but the elevation is so great that fogs and mist frequently fill the entire valley, and conceal the mountains around for days together, thus rendering in-door life desirable, if not imperative. As is usually the case in places where fogs and mist are present a great part of the time, the atmosphere is remarkably transparent and clear when they have lifted. Distance is almost annihilated, and the outlines of the surrounding Alps are clean-cut, and show superb effects of color, particularly at sunrise and sunset.

Our photograph shows us the newer and more substantially built portion of the little town, together with the church, a more pretentious building, perhaps, than the majority of Swiss villages possess. The brawling cataract passes down under the bridge to feed the River Reuss, and so finds its way into the Lake of Lucerne. The sharp, rocky peaks, partly concealed in mist, near the upper left-hand corner, belong to the Spitzberge, which rises to a height of over ten thousand feet.

17. Hospenthal and Andermatt.—The picture now before us gives a view of the Valley of Urseren, with a portion of the town of Hospenthal, looking back in the direction over which we have traveled from the Lake of Lucerne. Our photographer has gone up on a knoll back of the church, and made the view as nearly as possible at right angles to the one which has just left the screen. The pleasant little town of Andermatt can be seen just to the right of the roof of the transept of the church, with a long, straight stretch of road below leading in that direction. The very steep, rocky bluff on the mountain to the left of the church tower descends to the Urner Loch, or tunnel, of which we spoke a few moments ago ; the Devil's Bridge lying a little farther down to the left. A close look at that portion of the mountain that overlies the town of Andermatt will show a number of zigzag lines, which mark the ascent of the road on the Oberalp Route, as it is called. At least two thousand feet of ascent have to be made from the ridge of Andermatt before reaching the Oberalp Pass; this takes the traveler quite into the clouds, and it is seldom that these high latitudes are entirely free from some traces of them ; a large mass is seen resting on the top of the distant mountain, although the weather was exceptionally fine on the day when the view was made. The entrance to the Urner Loch, to which we before called attention, is a favorite gathering place for these clouds, which often boil up in immense masses from the cold, rocky bluffs near the Devil's Bridge, and ascend to join with others that, like those in the picture, constantly hang over the sharp pinnacles above.

18. **Berne.**—Our travels among the high moun-tains and lakes may now be agreeably varied by vis-

iting some of the beautiful towns—small cities they really are—which are situated rather towards the central portions of Switzerland.

The panoramic view of Berne now before us gives an excellent idea of the romantic surroundings and beautiful situation of the town—or at least a portion of it. The photographer has taken his stand on the high ground of the Altenberg, at a point which commands the beautiful sweep of the river Aar, which is crossed by two bridges. The further one, the Nydeckbrucke, is built largely of granite, is 900 feet long, and has a fine central span or arch 150 feet wide and 93 feet high, which we see very distinctly in the picture.

The better portions of Berne are built on a considerably higher level than that of the houses we see in the picture before us, and the great Nydeck bridge was constructed on this level to avoid the inconveniences of ascent and descent. Berne is the capital of the canton of the same name, which ranks second in size and first in population of all the cantons, or states, of Switzerland. Since the year 1849 it has been the seat of government. Most of the foreign ministers also reside here. The population of the city is 44,000.

To get a little better idea of this charming old place, let us imagine that we have crossed the Nydeck bridge and continued our walk a short dis- in the same direction.

19. The Street of Justice and Clock-Tower, Berne.—A very few moments from the bridge brings us to the interesting and picturesque view we now have before us. We are standing in the heart of the city, and on our way hither have observed the substantial, yet uncommon manner of building which prevails here. The houses on either side of the street are of stone throughout, and have arcades in the first story which connect and form a long, covered walk. The ground floors back of these arcades are devoted to shops of various kinds, which are deficient in light, as always happens in these situations. The bed of the street is a model of magnificent paving, as can be seen in the picture, and the cleanliness of the whole town is highly praiseworthy.

In the rear of one of the numerous water fountains with which this portion of the town is supplied, and which are very quaint in design, our photograph shows us the famous old clock-tower, with its large dial and turret above. The hours are struck on the gong in the open part of the turret by a figure that that can be seen on close examination, and there are quaint puppets of bears marching in procession, cocks crowing and flapping their wings, and Father Time with hour-glass and sceptre, which take a part in the striking of the clock, and always attract crowds of the idle and curious to witness it.

This curious old tower was one of the defences of the outer wall of the town, and was built in the twelfth century. Since that time, however, the town has increased in size until it now stands nearly in its centre.

20. The Hotel de Ville, Berne.—This pretty modern structure is in the southwestern portion of the city, and includes the different public offices and departments of the Swiss Legislature. The diet is composed of two bodies; the Standerath, which has two representatives from each of the twenty-two cantons of Switzerland, and the Nationalrath, which has one deputy or representative for every 20,000 inhabitants, or fraction over 10,000.

Before our departure from this pleasant city let us very briefly review its history and industries. Berne was founded in 1191 by Duke Berthold V., of Zahringen, and became a free city of the empire in 1218, and finally secured its independence in 1339. At one time, not long after this date, it was ruled by tyrannical patrician conservatives, and liberty was a thing unknown. The power fell from the grasp of this party never to return to it again in 1831. The armoral badge of Berne is the bear, the name having this signification in the old German language. There are always some fine specimens of this animal to be seen in the bear-pits, near the Nydeck bridge. The town has the enviable reputation of possessing the most numerous and best appointed charitable institutions of any in Europe. Besides the more usual industries followed in other cities of its kind, Berne is famous for its watch-making and wood-carving, being the centre of trade in these articles for the populous and busy canton of which it is the capital.

21. Panorama of Freiburg.—Our route to the Lake of Geneva leads us directly past the quaint town of Freiburg, so we will not pass it without a short visit. The panoramic view of the city now before us is seen from the railroad, aad is very striking. The city is seen to be finely situated on high ground above the R   Sarine, which is crossed by a graceful yet strong suspension bridge. By looking very closely we can see the immense sweep of the cables supporting the bridge, and which are 870 feet in length. This magnificent effort of engineering science was completed under the supervision of M. Chaley, of Lyons, in 1834.

It is almost an universal rule that towns which are famous for their picturesque situations are better looked at from a distance, and that too near an acquaintance with them reveals narrow quarters, crowded and dirty streets, and other unpleasant features. Freiburg is no exception to this rule, being very different from Berne, with its clean thoroughfares. After our visit to the latter town there is little to interest us in Freiberg except the cathedral, which we see occupying the centre of the picture, and can examine better from our present point of view than if we crossed over into the town. It is named for Saint Nicholas, and is a handsome specimen of Flamboyant-gothic architecture, having been commenced in 1285, and undergone the usual vicissitudes and restorations which seem to fall to the lot of these great monuments of religious art. The cathedral contains a very large and fine organ, said to be one of the finest in Europe; it was built by Aloys Moser, and has 7,800 pipes.

22. The Old Fountain, Freiburg.—Should we determine to brave the unpleasantnesses of the town and cross the bridge to have a closer look at it, we shall not do better than to walk a little on the outskirts, in the neighborhood of the old fortifications. The old fountain on the right is of about the same date as the remnants of the city wall, which we see leading up to the little white chapel in the middle of the view.

This picture takes us right in among the people, showing us how the fountain is the chief gathering-place for the neighborhood. In old towns like this the convenience of water-spigots in the houses is scarcely dreamed of; everybody coming to the fountain to obtain the supply of water needed for domestic uses, and, at times, bringing whatever vegetables are to be cooked for the day to the same place to wash them. Gossiping and news retailing here go on in plenty, and crowds of idle men and boys are always loafing about, as we see in the picture.

The old walls in this locality are quite well preserved, and are always full of interest to us who know of no such things as walled towns—at least in the ancient sense.

23. Geneva From Rousseau's Island.—We have now a few moments only in the city of Geneva, before starting on our sail up the lake of the same name. We feel that our time will be better spent on the water, enjoying the unrivalled scenery for which this sheet of water is so famous, than in the cities and towns to whose unpleasantnesses we have already alluded.

The city and lake of Geneva are probably familiar by name to almost everybody. Its beautiful situation on the outlet of the lake reminds us of Zurich, but things here are on a greater scale. The color of the water here is intensely blue, and its beauty was remarked upon by the poet Byron many years ago. Our view includes a block of fine buildings on the Quai du Mont Blanc, with the Hotel de Russie at the corner on the left, and a portion of the pretty little island called after the philosopher Rousseau, on the right. This island lies nearly in the middle of the swiftly flowing Rhone, and is approached by a short corridor from the Pont des Bergues, another fine bridge which crosses the river a short distance from the splendid Pont de Mont Blanc, at which we will soon get a closer look. In our present view it is seen in the middle distance.

No lovelier spot in which to spend an hour of a summer's morning can be imagined than this Island of Rousseau. We must not forget that the quai and bridge called by the name "Mont Blanc," command fine views of this great snow-peak, though distant nearly fifty miles. The mountain lies too far to the right to be seen in our picture, but we notice the presence of the tame swans, so common in these places, in a pool close down in the foreground of the view.

24. The New Bridge, Geneva.—Our present view is taken at not a very great distance from the preceding one. In the picture now before us, Rousseau's Island is in our rear. We observe a portion of one of the finely built blocks of houses which ornament this section of the city, and enough of the architecture of the bridge itself to see that it is a structure upon which first class workmanship has been expended.

But the chief interest of this picture, we need hardly say, is not in the immovable portions. We have taken special pains to reproduce the *movable* parts, which consist, as may easily be seen, of various sorts of water fowl, and numerous pigeons, that constantly fly about the bridge and settle on its piers. All of these birds are very tame, particularly the swans, which will come to any one for a morsel of bread. Four of them are floating near the point of the right-hand pier. The ducks, of course, appear much smaller, though there are more of them, and it is not very easy at first to tell which are ducks and which pigeons.

25. Nyon and the Chateau. Lake Geneva.—

Having in imagination shipped ourselves with our photographic apparatus on one of the comfortable lake steamers, we proceed up along the western shore and pass the pretty town of Nyon. We make an instantaneous view of it, for we have no time to stop. The waves and curious broken reflections on the water show how rapidly the picture has been taken. The camera has just been rested on the hand-rail of the boat for a moment while the instantaneous trigger is pulled.

Nyon dates from the time of the Romans, and several relics of this period are still to be seen here. They called it Colonia Julia Equestris, or Noviodunum. The ancient castle seen up on the hill, has walls ten feet in thickness. It was built in the twelfth century, or a little before the Castle of Chillon, where we shall arrive in a few moments, only making three stops, the first one of which is at

26. The Cathedral of Lausanne. Lake Geneva.

—The town of Lausanne is quite as old as Nyon, but is a much more important place, and presents an imposing appearance from the lake. It is the capital of the Canton de Vaud, and has a population of 30,000. It is noted for its excellent schools.

The cathedral, of which we here see the eastern end, is a fine building, dating from about the year 1270. It was consecrated in presence of Rudolph of Hapsburg by Pope Gregory X., and has been well restored by the late lamented Viollet-le-Duc. A discussion, celebrated in the local history, took place here in 1536. Viret, Farel and Calvin took part in it, and the result was that the Episcopal See was transferred to Freiburg, the Canton of Vaud was separated from the Church of Rome, and the supremacy of Savoy was overthrown. The interior contains a number of fine monuments. The terrace on which the cathedral stands commands a superb view of the lake.

A short walk into the town brings us to the house in which the celebrated Gibbon finished his great work entitled " History of the Decline and Fall of the Roman Empire."

27. The Market-Place, Vevey.—Continuing our sail not more than a dozen miles up the lake, we reach the charming town of Vevey. We here have a view of the market-place, and can see the every-day life of the people, which is an advantage only to be obtained by photography when used instantaneously.

A very ancient association or guild, whose object is the cultivation of the grapevine, is still in existence at Vevey. Those farmers who can show the best and most flourishing vineyards to the inspectors who are sent out every spring and fall, receive rewards of merit from the guild.

The association gives a festival about once in fifteen years, which is known as the *Fete des Vignerous.* Hundreds of persons take part in it. The wines made in this district are very good, and the steep hills on the lakeside, at which we shall get a closer look in our next view, are terraced to the height of hundreds of feet above the water with growing vines.

28. Inclined Railroad. Territet-Glion. Lake Geneva.—We are now almost at the head of this beautiful lake, and have not failed to observe how the almost flat banks of the lower part near Geneva have given place to higher and higher hillsides, some of them, like the one before us, being very steep.

The lakeside at this place is thickly populated, and in fact is an almost continuous village. A large population is also found in the small hamlets situated on the hills high above the lake, and far back from it. Glion is one of these, and the railroad leads directly to it; it is about 1200 feet above the water, and commands magnificent views over the lake in all directions. It is a favorite resort for travelers who desire to spend a short time in recuperating from the fatigues of continued change of place amidst beautiful scenery and in pure air. The construction of the railway has vastly increased the business of Glion, which was formerly a very quiet place, accessible only by carriage from Montreux, after a tedious ascent of nearly two hours.

The heat in summer here is very great. Even at such high elevations as Glion it is very trying. The peculiarities of soil and climate render this portion of Switzerland very well adapted for the cultivation of the grape, and excellent wines are made in this neighborhood. There is a "grape-cure" for invalids in the autumn. A close look at the view will show us the vines trained on their sticks, and pretty well covering the hillside.

29. The Castle of Chillon.—We shall have to proceed hardly a mile from our last stopping place before arriving at this famous castle ; after visiting which we must hurry on into the Bernese Oberland.

Our photograph gives us as satisfactory an idea of this world-renowned building as it is possible to obtain without actually going to the spot. Bearing in mind that we are on the lake shore, at the foot of the high, steep hills spoken of in connection with our last view, it will be easily understood that the whole situation and surroundings of the Castle of Chillon are pre-eminently picturesque and beautiful.

The castle is built on a rock which is nearly surrounded by deep water, although close to the shore. It was built by Amadeus IV. of Savoy, in 1238. It was long used as a prison, and it is stated on good authority that a number of persons connected with the Reformation in its earlier years were here confined. Byron's sonnet on Bounivard, the "Prisoner of Chillon," is doubtless familiar to almost everyone, and, as is usually the case with these efforts of literature which are primarily intended to work upon the emotions and sensibilities, the poem has but a very slender historical foundation. Great cruelties must have been practiced here, nevertheless. The "outliette" was a trap-door opening on a small stairway of three steps at the upper part of one of the castle towers. The prisoner, blindfolded, was instructed to walk downstairs and have the bandage removed from his eyes at the bottom. With the fatal belief that his deliverance was at hand, he would walk down the three steps and immediately fall an immense distance into the lake, his body being cut to pieces by knives set in the walls as it fell by them.

30. Interlaken and the Jungfrau.—Our entrance upon the glories of the Bernese Oberland may be very fittingly made from Interlaken, of which we have a view now before us. The town with its population of somewhat over four thousand, is a centre for tourists from all portions of the globe, and consists largely of hotels. Its situation, as seen in the picture, is very charming. The River Aare, which we observe close in the foreground, connects the two celebrated lakes of Thun and of Brienz. The name "Interlaken," or "Between the Lakes," is therefore a well-chosen one.

The majestic Jungfrau, the chief mountain of the Bernese Oberland range, is well seen in our view, and constitutes the chief feature of interest in the vicinity of Interlaken. Only that portion of the great peak that is covered by eternal snows can be seen in the picture. The lower wooded slopes being cut off from view by the rounded hill just below. It must not be forgotten that the view now before us includes a vast amount of subject; the distance to the summit of the Jungfrau being about twelve miles in a direct line, and the height of the same more than thirteen thousand feet. The precipitous slopes of the nearer hills, just below the summit, mark the entrance to the valley of Lauterbrunnen, and the large white spot at the foot of the rounded hill to the left is the Hotel Jungfraublick, celebrated for its fine view of the mountains. The sunset effects here are remarkably fine; the reflections of the rosy or golden light from the snows of the great peak illuminate everything that faces the mountain.

31. The Valley of Lauterbrunnen.—The word "Lauterbrunnen" means "nothing but brooks." Fanciful as it may seem to give such a name to a valley, the use of the term will be abundantly justified if a visit to the locality be made after a heavy rainstorm. As the photograph shows, the sides of the valley consist of very steep, rocky walls, and although there are numerous waterfalls there at almost all times, a smart rainfall at once changes the hillsides into literally "nothing but brooks."

The valley is a couple of miles long and about three-quarters of a mile wide. The "Staubbach," the most celebrated of the waterfalls, descends from an overhanging precipice nearly a thousand feet in height, and when mists float around the upper portions of the rocky walls, the sight of this cascade descending, apparently from the sky, is a very impressive one.

The distance hither from Interlaken is eight miles, and the ride is a succession of beautiful views. Like Grindlewald, the little town of Lauterbrunnen is a great centre for tourists, and is overrun with peddlers and beggars, among whom we frequently observe the unsightly *goitre*, a swelling of the glands in the neck, which sometimes grows so large as to hang down over the breast. The beautiful carved woodwork, for which Switzerland has so long been famous may be had here in plenty.

The mountains seen at the upper end of the valley are a continuation of the Jungfrau range, to which we are now very near.

32. The Wetterhorn From Grindlewald.—The usual route from the Valley of Lauterbrunnen to the Valley of Grindlewald lies over the famous Wengern Alp. All travelers agree that this excursion is unrivalled in Switzerland for the views it affords of the Jungfrau and of its glaciers. The descent from the summit of the Wengern Alp is very interesting, and the great mass of the Wetterhorn, which we have here in the picture before us is a prominent feature in the extensive prospect.

Grindlewald has much the same general character as Lauterbrunnen. It is a great centre for tourists from all parts of the world, and in the summer months is an exceedingly busy place. The native population numbers about three thousand. The traveler on arriving at Grindlewald feels that he is in the heart of the Alps, and the views are indeed stupendous. The Wetterhorn, which forms the subject of our picture, rises to a height of 12,149 feet— almost equalling the Jungfrau. Other enormous mountain masses, scarcely inferior in elevation, bound the southern portion of the valley and shut in the view. Excursions from Grindlewald have to be made either by mule or by " chaise-a-porteur," a sort of litter, on which persons are carried in a sitting posture. There is only one wagon road, and this leads back to Lauterbrunnen.

The glaciers of Grindlewald formerly had a great reputation, and indeed are still interesting, as we shall see in a moment; but they have partaken in that general shrinkage in the size of all the Swiss glaciers, which has been so noticeable in the past few years. A small portion of the Upper Glacier of Grindlewald is seen in the picture near the foot of the mountain to the right; but the one we shall now examine is situated still farther around to the right, at the base of the Mettenberg.

33. The Glacier of Grindlewald.—We here have a view of the lower one, which descends in a gloomy ravine between the Mettenberg and the Eiger.

A few very brief remarks upon these great natural wonders may not be out of place. The picturesque charm of Alpine scenery is much increased by these masses of ice descending into the beautiful, cultivated · fields. The great eternal snow region is far above, and may be considered as the material or supply from which the glacier is formed. It is well known that glacier ice is different in structure from ordinary ice. The alternations between the sun's heat and the freezing that sets in again during the night, are believed to gradually change the loose, powdery snow of the higher altitudes into ice. The thickness of the glaciers is difficult to estimate, but it is believed in many cases to be several hundred feet, at least.

There are somewhat more than four hundred and fifty glaciers in the Swiss Alps. The one before us is remarkable for having descended to the lowest point of any of them, having on one occasion reached the very low level of 3,500 feet above the sea. The next lowest were the two great glaciers at Chamounix, which came down to 3,660 feet.

Having now had a good look at the outside of a Swiss glacier, we will proceed to examine *its interior*.

34. Tunnel in the Glacier of Grindlewald.—It has been a custom for many years to cut tunnels several hundred feet long directly into the glacier-

ice. As the view shows, there is ample space for two
or more persons to walk abreast, and the path is
made of two rows of stout planks, on which walking
is quite easy, even for ladies and children or infirm
persons.

Although many people experience a feeling of fear
at the idea of thus walking into the immense ice-field,
which is constantly cracking and making noises of
various kinds, it is not of long duration. The novelty
and interest of the situation soon dissipate any want
of confidence, and the entire attention is taken up
in admiring the splendid color of the clean, pure ice,
which is an opalescent, pearly green. A lengthened
sojourn in the tunnel is not unpleasant. The temperature is not excessively low ; there is always more or
less melting going on in summer. A little stream of
the ice-water can be seen in the upper right-hand
corner of the view.

Our photograph has been made from a point far
inside of the tunnel, looking out towards the entrance.
Let us ask our friends in the audience to try and
realize the beauty of these pale, icy walls, which our
photograph, good as it is, can only reproduce in
monochrome.

35. Entrance to the Via Mala.—Our route now
takes us through the grandest and most picturesque
mountain pass or defile in Switzerland. The name
"Via Mala," or "bad road" is a relic of savage
times, when the splendid post-roads which now inter-
sect the country everywhere were undreamed of. In
fact, so late as the year 1822 the Via Mala was a mere
path some four feet in width, which followed the left
bank of the stream the whole way. We must further

remark that the view now before us shows the actual commencement of the famous pass known as the Splugen ; the road making a rapid, yet evenly graded ascent from Thusis, a pleasant village just in the rear of the spot where the photographer stood when making the picture. The scenery is exceedingly grand, and is on an immense scale ; a close examination of our picture reveals the broad carriage-road near the bottom of the hill, in shadow, on the right, and a somewhat narrower one curving amongst the trees on the other side of the river. The enormous bluff of rock which fills up the left hand portion of the view is known as the Johannsberg, and rises eight hundred feet from the Rhine below. The river at this point describes a number of very graceful curves, as the picture shows, finally straightening itself out, as it were, to flow along through the meadow land below Thusis, after being pent up for many miles in the rocky chasms and gorges of the Via Mala.

The rugged and precipitous character of the Via Mala is preserved throughout its entire length, the great bluff at the entrance being thrown into insignificance by those farther up the defile.

36. The Johannsberg, Via Mala.—The view now before us gives a somewhat better and more extended prospect. We are now looking in a direction opposite to our previous picture, which was taken from a point just beyond the wooded hill on the left, and looking this way.

The village of Thusis is distinctly seen in the centre of the view, at the foot of the precipitous Johannsberg. Little glimpses of the river Rhine and of the

carriage-road are there also, between the rock and
the steep hill on the left. The slopes of the Heinzen-
berg close in the view in the background.

  A close inspection of the summit of the Johannsberg, just where the great rocks form a sort of right
angle, will reveal some ruins of a castle known as
Hohen Rhaetien, or Hoch Realta. These ruins are
the oldest in all Switzerland, and occupy a most picturesque and commanding position. Their foundations stand at a height of eight hundred and seven
feet above the river, and in earlier days the castle
must have been impregnable. The other side of the
Johannsberg is quite as precipitous as the one seen
in the view, and even the grassy slopes on the near
side lead to other heights that no human foot can
scale. The only approach is from a village far
around to the right, and the pathway is so narrow
and steep that a few brave men could easily prevent
the ascent of a large force. The view from these
ruins surpasses description, and embraces a large
tract of the level country to the north, besides a considerable portion of the Via Mala.

  The village of Thusis, the meeting point of several
roads, is situated on high ground just beyond the
entrance of the gorge. Cool air from the great ravine
makes the temperature delightful even on the hottest
days.

  37. Splugen.—Our way up the celebrated Splugen Pass, which takes its name from the little town
seen in the picture, leads us the entire length of the
Via Mala ; some four miles or more. The peculiar
character of this great mountain gorge consists in
precipitous cliffs, which in some places approach each

other so closely that the daylight is dimmed, and render all efforts of the photographer to transcribe them, vain.

We finally emerge from the gloomy defile into the pretty, and yet rather bleak mountain valley, where the town of Splugen stands at the foot of the picturesque Kalkberg, which we see before us in the rear of the village. We have made a considerable ascent since leaving Thusis. The town of Splugen stands at an elevation of nearly five thousand feet above sea-level, and is the joining point of two chief Alpine passes—the Bernardino and the Splugen. The latter pass, properly speaking, begins at the town and crosses the summit about two thousand feet higher up. It is a very ancient one, and was known to the Romans; it was also highly dangerous until the construction of the new road by the Austrian Government in the year 1823. The zigzags by which the road ascends, and the avalanche or snow tunnels remind us of other Alpine passes.

Beyond its picturesque position, there is little or nothing of interest in the town. It formerly belonged to the lords of Sax; it was badly damaged by a flood in 1834. The River Rhine runs in front of the town, and vehicles cross it on a fine modern bridge, built of iron. The neighborhood offers a number of interesting walks and drives, both ascending to the summit, where the Italian custom-house is situated, and back in the direction of Thusis, through the Via Mala.

38. Entrance to the Stelvio Pass.—Although the Stelvio Pass lies just outside the border-line of Switzerland, we have given a view of its Italian side here, owing to the peculiarities it presents in its rocky, mountainous walls.

The Stelvio is the highest pass in Europe over which vehicles can be driven. The column on the summit near the little refuge used by the laborers on the road gives the elevation above the sea at 9,045 feet, at the same time marking the boundary between Italy and the Austrian Tyrol.

Our view is made at a point on the Italian side, about a mile below the Baths of Bormio. The large hotel is distinctly seen under the sharp rocky peak at the right, and the cluster of little houses forming the town can also be distinguished slightly to the left and lower down. The Stelvio road ascends in zigzags on the hill at the right, and pursues its way up the gloomy looking valley in the background.

Bormio stands in a vale opening directly into the Val Tellina, where there is considerable industry in wines. Thus the rides in both directions are very interesting, but it may be doubted whether the Stelvio is the equal of some of the other Swiss passes, so far as scenery is concerned ; although there are very fine views to be had of the great Ortler group of mountains.

39. Schloss Stockalper and the Rhone Valley. —Our route takes us now into some of the less stupendous and exciting, but none the less interesting portions of Switzerland. The region near the little town of Brieg, where our view is made, may seem tame after the gloomy mountain fastnesses and the rocky walls of the Stelvio and Via Mala. But it is a fact universally agreed upon by travelers, that a too long continued sojourn in the higher mountain districts becomes fatiguing both to the mind and to the eye. The interest and surprise which are excited by the first views of precipitous mountains close at hand, become actually painful if the traveler be subjected to the impression for a lengthened time, and the first views of the open country, where the eye has more space in which to range with freedom, will be welcomed with delight.

The most passing glance at our view will show, however, that we have not taken our friends into a flat country, the mountains upon either side of the valley being of considerable height, and snow being plainly visible on the one in the rear, just to the left of the tower. The river Rhone lies rather too far to the right to be seen in the view, but it runs a rapid course through the lovely intervale back of the town, and turns abruptly to the right on its way to the Lake of Geneva at the point of the hill in the centre of the picture.

The little town of Brieg, of which we see a large portion in the view, is beautifully situated, and has a rather more imposing appearance than most of the other towns in this vicinity, owing to the numerous steeples and towers on its larger houses, as well as those of Schloss Stockalper, at which we will now take a closer look.

40. Schloss Stockalper, Brieg.—This view will be immediately recognized as having been taken from a point nearer to the castle or Schloss than the preceding one. The three large stone towers are seen to be the same, but their positions are somewhat changed. The little glimpses through the towers and around the castle give an idea of the loveliness of the rural scenery of this part of Switzerland, and a part of a fine double row of poplar trees which line the post-route is also to be seen.

This town is an excellent centre for excursions. By following the boldly-rising hill on the right for some half-dozen hours, the great Aletsch Glacier is reached; while by ascending on the other side of the valley from Brieg we are soon in the steep inclines of the Simplon Pass.

The Stockalper family, to whom the half-ruined castle here seen formerly belonged, were at one time wealthy and powerful. A tall tower at Gondo, very similar to the three seen in the view was built there by the Stockalpers as a refuge for travelers, before the roads were either opened or in safe condition. The castle stands, as can be seen, on the rise of a small hill, which makes it a very prominent feature in the land-scape for miles around. Our previous view showed the town, which is beautifully situated to the right of the old castle. It thus, as it were, stands guard over the town on the south.

There is little or nothing of interest in the town itself, with the exception of some rather picturesque turreted houses. Brieg is the terminus of the rail-road. The lovely situation of the town, and the numerous excursions, however, quite make up for this deficiency.

41. Swiss Chalets at Naters.—A charming walk of not more than a mile across the Rhone from Brieg, brings us to the quaint little village of Naters, which consists almost throughout of the picturesque chalets as seen in the view.

In making the delightful excursion to the Aletsch Glacier from Brieg, Naters is the first village passed through. It is interesting to botanists as being the last point in the Rhone Valley where the chestnut tree grows. The ascent from Naters in every direction is so steep that the air soon becomes too cold to allow the tree to flourish.

Naters is inhabited by a very poor class of people. The interiors of these houses are often wretched in the extreme, and correspond with their filthy exteriors. They are substantially constructed, however, as may be seen from the straight lines of the walls, and the solid manner in which the joists are mortised together. An ascending line of these mortises is seen just to the right of the small balcony under which the man and woman are standing. The whiter portions of the buildings consist of a sort of rubble or concrete work, the shapeless stones being strongly connected with mortar, which is afterwards plastered over on the outside. The manner in which these buildings are huddled together shows how valuable ground is in Switzerland. The village churchyard here is so small that all the dead bodies—or what is left of them—are removed once every ten years, the ground being dug completely over. The bones are placed in a charnel-house or "ossuary," attached to the church. This is a common custom in Switzerland.

42. The Morteratsch Glacier.—We shall not apologize for presenting another picture of one of the great Swiss glaciers, knowing how interesting they are in all their portions. It will be immediately noticed that the one before us gives a view of a differ-

ent part of the glacier formation from what we have
hitherto seen. The part now seen in the photograph
shows the actual end or bottom of the glacier, where
the water escapes from under the ice, and also the
manner in which huge pieces crack and still remain
in position for a long time before falling. The crack
in the ice over the arch is plainly seen, while far back
under the arch are other large masses which have
already fallen and are melting—very slowly indeed,
for the water of course is "ice-water" in the truest
sense of the term.

The rushing stream here represents the gathering
together of the liquid portions of the glacier; in
reality the water is as opaque as the thickest cream
from the detritus of the rocks that it has taken up when
low down near the bottom of the ice-mass. But when
we mount on the back of the glacier, and walk up a
little distance where we can look down into a cre-
vasse where the ice is clean and pure, we there find
the glacier-water running in streams of exquisite
purity and much the bluish-green color of the ice
itself.

43. The Gorner Glacier.—The little village of
Zermatt is generally visited for the sake of the fine
views to be had of the noble Matterhorn, which
rises to the height of 14,000 feet above the sea, but
this is by no means the only attraction of the neighborhood. Some of the finest glaciers in Switzerland
are easily accessible from Zermatt, and we here have
a view of the famous Gorner Glacier, which is seen
when we ascend the "Gorner Grat," as it is called,
the latter being a continuation of the Riffelberg.
The excursion up the Riffelberg is a justly favorite

one, and is easily made from the town. The majestic
glacier descends from the side of the Monte Rosa, a
portion of which is seen in the view. Like others
of its kind, it is reached by a steep slope or descent
from the rocks above, and at the point where our
picture has been taken it presents a jagged structure,
not unlike the Mer de Glace at Chamounix, though
not so regular and wave-like.

Interesting as the glacier itself is, the glorious panorama of cloud-piercing snowy peaks seen from the
little inn which can just be distinguished in the lower
left-hand corner of the picture, is still more attractive,
and is one of the most imposing in the Alps. The
enormous snowy shoulders of Monte Rosa and the
Lyskamer, and the colossal rocks of the Breithorn are
in full view, and we frankly admit that nothing we
have yet seen gives us a better idea of the wondrous
mountain architecture and icy fields of the higher Alps.
It must not be forgotten that we are now standing at
an elevation of more than ten thousand feet. At the
foot of the glacier, a little below the spot where our
view is made, the ice formerly ran into the meadows,
so that the grass and the ice almost came into contact
with one another ; in fact, it rather encroached upon
them, but after the year 1867, it partook in the general shrinkage observed in the glaciers throughout
Switzerland.

44. The Hospice of St. Bernard and Mont Velan.
—There is a certain amount of similarity in the
principal Swiss passes, so we will only devote time
enough to the Great St. Bernard to take a look at the
celebrated hospice, or refuge, which we here see in
the photograph before us.

The Hospice of St. Bernard consists of two large buildings directly in the mountain pass of that name, and stands at an elevation of 8,120 feet; we see them plainly near the centre of the picture. One of these buildings contains the church, the rooms of the brotherhood, and other rooms for travelers; the other one contains lodgings for very poor wayfarers, store-houses, etc. No charge is made for the entertainment of travelers, but every one is expected to deposit in the alms-box a sum at least the equal of what he would pay in any ordinary hotel.

The St. Bernard dogs can still be seen here, but it is asserted that the genuine breed is extinct; many lives have been saved by these noble animals.

The expenses of this excellent charity are increasing, and it is a sad commentary on the meanness of human nature, when we say that the sum actually contributed by travelers who could well afford to pay a proper price for their accommodation, has not reached one-twentieth of what it should have done.

In the background we see the snow-covered Mont Velan. Its summit is more than 12,000 feet above sea-level, and is very difficult to climb to.

45. Chamounix and Mont Blanc.—The little village of Chamounix, consisting almost entirely of hotels, is famous the world over, and if the visitor has even passably good weather he will not be disappointed. On a bright, clear morning the panorama of Mont Blanc, with the great glaciers of Bossons and the Mer de Glace, and the different "aiguilles," or needles, as the French people call the sharp rocky points surrounding them, form a picture that will never be forgotten. Nor is it only in clear weather

that the traveler will be thus rewarded. It sometimes happens, in summer particularly, that a thun-
der-cloud will envelop the bases of the mountains,
allowing now and then a bit of some rocky peak or
snow-covered summit to be seen in isolated majesty in
the sky, as it were, while the forked lightning flashes
and strikes far below. If the sun appears before the
conclusion of the storm, the sight becomes one of
the grandest that the eye of man can behold. At
such a time the ice-covered mountains, gorgeous in
their coloring, freshened by the rain, will be seen
through the impalpable prismatic curtain of the
rainbow.

Our photograph shows the summit of Mont Blanc
on a clear morning, the high, rounded point over
the hotel at the left, and the Dome and the Aiguille
du Gouter farther to the right. The Glacier des
Bossons, at which we shall soon get a nearer look, is
also seen descending from near the summit for almost
its entire length.

**46. Diligence on the Route Between Cham-
ounix and Geneva.**—This picture gives us an excellent idea of the manner in which passengers and
baggage are conveyed between the two principal
points mentioned. The diligences in other parts of
Switzerland are built on a different plan.

The road between Geneva and Chamounix is a
superb effort of engineering skill, and the peculiar
form of the diligence, as seen in the view, has doubtless been settled upon as well suited to the wide,
even, and well-graded ascent. It will be observed
that the seats for the passengers are all arranged on
top of the coach, except the three in the coupe, as it

is called, the window of which is seen just above the
fore-wheel and under the driver, who is also seen in
his place with the reins in his hand. The horses are
attached in a rather original manner; two being
placed side by side as usual, next the body of the
coach, but in advance of them there are three har-
nessed side by side. The third horse in our picture
is concealed from view by the bodies of the others, a
small portion only of his legs and feet being visible
on the side next the houses. A glance at the left
side of the picture shows the porters in the act of
loading luggage in the interior or body of the coach,
which occupies the whole of the space in the rear of
the coupe. This arrangement brings so much weight
low down, that even when all the seats above are
occupied the coach is well balanced, and there is no
risk of an overturn. The curtains at the sides can
be drawn to in case of rain, and in fine weather nothing is in the way to intercept the splendid views on
the route.

47. The Mer de Glace, Chamounix.—Of all the
short excursions in the neighborhood of the town of
Chamounix, the one to the Montanvert is the most
delightful. An easy ascent of about two and a half
hours brings the traveler to the inn, where a comfortable luncheon may be had, and the magnificent view
of the Mer de Glace, which we here have on the
screen before us, enjoyed at leisure.

The Mer de Glace, or "sea of ice," to translate the
name literally, is very properly so called. The cre-
vasses in the ice are so deep, and the projecting
crests so bold that the resemblance to a frozen sea is
striking. This great glacier descends from the chain

of mountains of which Mont Blanc is the highest peak. In the view before us the lower part of the glacier is shown, with the peaks of the Grandes Jorasses in the background.

Tourists as a rule cross the Mer de Glace to an inn on the other side, known as the Chapeau.· Persons are ready to supply creepers for the shoes and other affairs to prevent the feet from slipping on the ice. With these precautions taken and a good guide to lead the way, the excursion is quite free from risk, and is just of a pleasant length ; an hour and a half is generally occupied in crossing. Admirable opportunities are thus afforded to those interested in glaciers to become well familiarized with a world-renowned one at a small expenditure of money and time.

Everything, of course, depends upon the condition of the weather when making these excursions in the mountains, but it is well to remember that on cloudy days, when the scud hangs over the higher peaks, they are not devoid of interest to those who are content to see a little of Nature in all her phases.

48. Ice Pyramids on the Glacier des Bossons, Chamounix.—The Glacier des Bossons is the lower one of the two great ice-fields which descend into the beautiful valley of Chamounix. The ravine in the mountain side through which this great glacier comes down is very rough, and the surface of the ice is inclined at a steeper angle than the Mer de Glace, besides which it is much more broken and irregular.

Our picture shows some of these surface irregularities, which here take the form of pyramids or "aiguilles." The view has been taken at a considerable height above the valley. The diligence route to

Geneva can be seen as a long white line, running along in the valley on this side of the river. The camera has been set on a high point and directed downwards in making this view, which accounts for the somewhat unusual effect of perspective.

A beautiful specimen of the aiguille, or needle-shaped ice-pyramid is seen at the extreme right of the picture. The term "aiguille" is chiefly applied to rocks and mountain peaks, but the slender sharpness of the formation we speak of fully justifies the use of the word; it is really as sharp as a needle.

49. Murren.—Some of the most interesting views of the great mountains of Switzerland are to be obtained by ascending the foot-hills or lower eleva-tions. This is especially the case in places like the Bernese Oberland, where the mountains are charac-terized by great steepness as well as height.

The view now on the screen gives a portion of the splendid Alpine panorama seen from Murren, an humble village which stands on a sort of rocky shelf at the top of the precipice overlooking the valley of Lauterbrunnen. We see the small chalets of which the village is composed, in the foreground. The black spots on the roofs are stones, which are put there to keep them steady during the fierce winds that sometimes prevail in these upper regions.

The precipitous sides of the Schwarze Mönch, and the snow-covered sides of the Eiger and Mönch, which are partly concealed by mist, can be plainly· seen. The roof of the hotel can be made out at the extreme right-hand end of the village, just under the steeply-inclined peak of the Eiger. The Jungfrau, the monarch of the range, lies behind the Schwarze

Mönch, and too far to the left to be visible in the view.

50. Mont Blanc.—Our trip through Switzerland is now concluded, but we have reserved for our last view in this beautiful land a picture which we are sure will dwell in the minds of our friends with a force and persistency only second to the impressions made by an actual survey of the glories which are there to be seen.

Our photograph has been taken from an elevated standpoint on the Tete Noire route, looking back over the valley of Chamounix, and commanding an unobstructed view of the Mont Blanc chain of mountains. The great height at which we are standing is testified to by the patches of snow seen near the middle of the picture. The long, sweeping black line just beyond the snow, marks the beginning of a steep descent into the valley of Chamounix, and slightly to the left of its middle we observe a large white spot, which closer examination shows to be an hotel of considerable size. Our photographer has so chosen his point of view that this hotel becomes a prominent object in the picture, and serves to convey some slight idea of the immense scale on which the surroundings have been reproduced. The summit of Mont Blanc is at the very top of this picture nearly in the middle, and we also see the different points remarked upon when we were in the Valley of Chamounix—the Dome and the Aiguille du Gouter and the Glacier des Bossons among others. We can now easily understand how this majestic landscape inspired the poet Coleridge to write,

"Hast thou a charm to stay the morning star
In his steep course? So long he seems to pause
On thy bald awful head, O sovran Blanc."